HISTORY OF THE LION FAMILY

By Ghuntas Kaur

History of the Lion Family

ISBN 978-1-7397401-6-0

Printed in the United Kingdom by
KhalisHouse Publishing

www.KhalisHouse.com
info@KhalisHouse.com

Find us on:
Instagram/KhalisHouse

Preface

At the heart of *History of the Lion Family* lies a story of discrimination within and outside the Sikh and Punjabi communities. This discrimination manifests itself in many forms including wealth disparities, conflicting gender dynamics, religious prejudice and – mostly consequently – the genocide of an entire group of people. However, discrimination is not an isolated event that affects one individual at one moment in time. *History of the Lion Family* delves deep into the scars that trauma lies on families and how it carries through the generations.

Thus, it is not a story that I alone am responsible for. In fact, the story predominantly is that of my forebears. My grandfathers and grandmothers kick this journey off to a start with their experiences in the 1980s. My parents take the mantle for the 2000s with their story of adapting to the Canadian lifestyle while handling the expectations of their community. Finally, I cover my own generation from a perspective of reflection on our history. All poems are based on true stories of my family or people in the Sikh and Punjabi communities.

In both India and Canada, there is a stigma about discussing our traumatic experiences. This phenomenon stems from the oppression of opinions that was prevalent in 1980s India. Discussing the atrocities occurring to you and your family potentially would have been met with jail time, brutality or death. Therefore, children and grandchildren were taught to keep opinions caged. *History of the Lion Family* aims to break those systematic barriers and give a pen to my family's experiences and the intergenerational trauma that remains.

Contents

Preface i

1984: The First Generation 4

    PYRES OF THE NIGHT 5

    SHOELACE NOOSE 6

    SHOTGUN AND A BOTTLE OF RUM 8

    THE LESSER FIVE 10

    STAINED FINGERTIPS 11

    TRAIN TO LAHORE 12

    THE SEARCH 14

    TEA 15

    A BLANK SPACE 18

    A MAN WITH A SWORD IS NO SAVIOR 19

    ART SHOP 20

    RED 21

    OPIUM HEART 22

    DELUSIONS OF PRIVILEGE 23

    SEVEN SIBLINGS 25

    WHO ARE THE SCUTTLING RATS? 26

    NUMBERS DON'T COLLUDE WITH VICTORY
.... 27

    IN THE NAME OF GANDHI 28

    TIMELINE 29

    HAIR 30

    SOUL OF PUNJAB 31

2001: The Mussalmans 32

    MAPS 33

CANADIAN TAX 34

THE YOUNG PRINCES 35

PRICE OF BLOOD 37

PAINT ME WITH THE COLOURS OF THE
RAINBOW 38

CAST ME IN A PLAY 39

WHITE SEA 41

LITTLE INDIA 43

LANGAR HALL 44

ADRIFT PAPERS TO GLUE 45

WHERE ELSE, IF NOT HOME 46

ELECTRICAL FAILURES 47

NEWSPAPER CLIPPINGS 48

ARRANGED 49

BOUQUET OF BLACK ROSES 51

SIGNATORY OF MAN'S COUNTRY 52

CHANDIGARH 53

BOOK TOMB 54

IRON BRANDING OR ROPE HANGING 55

GALI FLOODS 56

PROMOTIONS 57

THE GARBAGE MAN 60

2020: The Canadians 61

SILENCE SONGS 62

WAIT FOR HER TO STAND 63

OLD RIVERS FLOW IN BLOOD 64

TEXTBOOK ANSWERS 65

PROPORTIONS 66

NOVEMBER 11TH 67

GHUNTAS 68

KHALISTAN... 70

MIGHTY.. 71

CHANDIGARH, PART 2 72

DREAMING OF DELHI................................. 73

SUNDIALS... 74

THE MOOSE CRAZE 75

SOURCE MATERIAL 77

SOCIAL SCALE.. 78

SILK SHACKLES.. 80

THE CRIMES OF MOTHERS' MOUTHS 81

FAMILY BUSINESS...................................... 82

DIZZY SPELLS... 83

TWO PEAS OUT OF A POD 84

TO MY FATHER... 86

PTSD 89

Bonus Content 90

ਟੁੱਟੀ ਪੰਜਾਬੀ... 90

ਖਾਲੀ ਅਲਮਾਰੀ 95

1984: The First Generation

On June 1st, Operation Blue Star was initiated by Indira Gandhi which resulted in the attack of Sikhi's holiest site, Sri Harminder Sahib (The Golden Temple). The subsequent Sikh genocide perpetuated by the government's anti-Sikh sentiments ended the year with 20,000 Sikh casualties.

sheets of iron rain
slivers of proud hearts praying
golden gates stand strong

PYRES OF THE NIGHT

You slave away
in the factory
Building the tyres that hunt us
Watching coworkers drop dead
   one by one

until the only one left on the assembly line
   is you
with hair cut long ago
in a cover-up that worked

The two boys
of the last guru
revered in martyrdom
were encased in brick
Their cement our kerosene
and just the same
we make the last stand in these tyres
Rubber burning through the night
a testament to faith

SHOELACE NOOSE

Dangling shoes tied around her neck
Soles of dirt
   souls of black
The ones that the women crudely coloured in
showing her caste and her religion

Pushed through the crowd
Shoved hand to hand
Those who touch the coal cringing
yet reaching back for more
Not resisting mockery at the expense of
a sixteen year old girl
So a parade the spectacle makes
Women cheering from windows
Wearing gowns that don't quite
match their declared prestige

One woman
– both a sister and daughter –
films from above
Capturing
the naked figure
   bare feet
   shorn head
Those soles clapping
against one another
Cheering
   Jeering

at what men
– both brothers and sons –
did to a girl

She stumbles through
pushed and shoved
Her body
not just sore
but abrasively battered
Silent and defeated
but her mind roars
Begging for
the laces to tighten

SHOTGUN AND A BOTTLE OF RUM

A small skeleton of a home
Singular room for five
Thin stairs leading to a bare top
Cows loitering where a kitchen should be

Beyond the five foot wall
fireworks go off
celebrating a students death
– just down the street
There the body still lies
Glimpsed on by your daughter
None to bury a rotting corpse
as former neighbours hide away
So it continues to rot away
to be seen
by adults and children alike

The night rings red
and you lie with a bottle of rum
and a shotgun to keep company
Protecting
Guarding
Awaiting for police to barge in
creep up those thin stairs
shake the roof
rouse the sleeping cows

All whilst your wife protects

a daughter and sons
from nightmares that choose
to strike the midnight clock

THE LESSER FIVE

They asked for five hundred
instead of five thousand
and you went on your knees in thanks
They sat next to you on the manja
Saying they want to
catch up with an old friend
You believing it was a place of safety
instead of simply a four-legged bed

They joked around
how men can't follow instructions
You forgetting who's instructions they were
Believing a colleague was next to you
complaining of a rough day at work

Consistently believing gangs
were groups of low-bred men
Instead of a leader's puppets in
a game of drugs and desperation

STAINED FINGERTIPS

Counting coins all day
Bags of thousands disappearing
behind locked cabinets
The keys hanging
only on one chain

Elders up front
now retired and allowed
to sit and collect checks
Smiling and showing off merchandise
in the form of patients and staff

Lecturing teachers to clean
and serve food
while sipping their third cup of tea
Paychecks not coming from clocked time
rather the skill of convincing people
to stain their fingers
by signing names on dotted lines
or with the grime remaining from
counting coins that disappear

TRAIN TO LAHORE

I stroll through the thin aisle
Stepping on bodies atop one another
Passing rows of beds
which should hold crouched figures
avoiding legs hanging over

Shadows slither behind me
My stench pungent in the air
but reaping waits for no one
So I crouch down
to run a finger down a little girls hair
Plait of three strands running over
a gaping shoulder
I kick a machete to the side
to pat a man's back
who slouches atop his wife
Commendable effort
alas not enough

I tap the barred windows
regretting that they weren't covered up
These folks never rode for a view
Lack of sunlight an easy tradeoff
As for me
asphyxiation is
less of a mess to wade through

Perhaps I should go pull the lever

before it passes through a town
carrying that stench to it's rivers
Giving a fright
to children that wait for the return
A waste of my energy certainly
for once this one is emptied
the next will be just as full
even knowing I'm the only one
left to linger these halls

THE SEARCH

Do you know your neighbour's hiding spot?
Having passed it wandering on by
Eyes respectfully drifting over it
trying to forgive the chance find

Is it in the cabinet cutting into the kitchen
or the cellar lying under the rug
Perhaps it's in the closet near the bedroom
just big enough for their five year old

Have you compared it to your own?
Imagining the scenarios
If you were over for tea
If your child needed refuge
or if you need to tell the others
Exchanging secrets to keep
your own hidden below the earth

Do you know your neighbour's hiding spot?
Did you chance upon it or search?

TEA

A spoon clinks on aunt's cracked pot
Bubbles pop in the boiling water
Sugar rushes from it's woolen sack
The faint accompaniment to woman's art

"Grab the leaves" Aunt says to her daughter
"They're only over there"
 right next to the flour
Meena's face appears above mine
Just a moment it seems to whisper

Why must I wait
among the dusty fumes of wood
Lying my head on the sack of flour
Legs cramping from my crumpled form

The women's voices echo through the wooden gap
"Damn neighbours with their damn troubles"
Aunt providing a soothing balm to Meena's growl
"Weeds attach when the weather shows turmoil
 A farmer's worth is only as big as his crop"
A CRACK sounds from my mother's rolling pin above

I know the Chaudhry's daughter
Her nimble hands the best at braiding our long hair
I don't remember her family having trouble
The fields we run through seemingly rich in their green

"Well, the weather seems nice"
Meena comments
An incessant tapping starts up
My mother's leather sandals an inch beyond our barrier
        providing a lullaby for eventual drift
Knock, knock, knock
    inviting me to widen the slight gap in the wood
How much longer must I wait

Cinnamon floods the air
        adding to the warm scent of aunt's tea
Why offer it to the guests
they would only leave when the leaves were seen
Knock, knock, knock
        The light from the gap fades

A sudden cacophony of voices rouse me from rest
Hands slapping knees and patting backs echoing
        the clear sign of men signaling their exit
There is a creak from our metal gate
Arms cradle me into warm embraces
Sun still setting in the distance
Mother finally returning from her daily errands
        Busy since the morn
It was not too late to play with the neighbour's daughter

Instead, I'm sent up to bed
It is not till many years later that I am told
the fields were not safe that day
with the armed men still lining the stone walls

As they did in that kitchen
watching women complete their dutiful art

A BLANK SPACE

Here I leave a blank

It's for those who deserve
the scrapes of their dignity intact

Don't divulge it full
by the gaping horror of crimes
Unable to be undone
yet unable to be forgotten

Don't plaster the pages
with the names of the faceless
Those that already chose to drop skin
for the costumes the night stages

Criminal sharks and sea snakes
captured in print
Filling a reserved empty net
somehow escaping

A MAN WITH A SWORD IS NO SAVIOR

He looks around him
with blood soaking into clothes of
fallen men
A sword slashing
into his neighbour's abdomen

He sees
Blood
Violence
War
All the idioms
that philosophers
push disdain towards
That people mock
from the safety
of their shingled homes

This warrior also sees
Brothers at arms
Loyalty
in its truest form
He sees fathers
husbands
sons
Willing to fight
Risk their lives
for the lives of innocents

ART SHOP

I walked into a shop
There was a small corner
reserved just for us

There I saw precise lines
depicting the martyrs
Halos surrounding the ones
we were to place above our furniture

Right next to them
I saw misplaced
blank canvases
sitting among the masterpieces

A store clerk saw what I
was pondering and
she told me
they were right at home
Art in their own right

For they were donated by
a mother
who's son put aside the paintbrush
to die

RED

Lamb's veins
A butcher's apron
Painted doorways

Lion's veins
Edge of a sword
Honour and courage

Cobblestones
AN ALTAR
Wax with wick
Pictures of martyrs
awash with romance

Battlefield
Temples in the ruin
A river
full of temper and shame

Wrists of a woman
Her husband's neck
Tears among fire
Ash with berry dye
indistinguishable
in the desert dust

OPIUM HEART

Lines of infection drawn
on the bell shaped land
Stretching into
the states around
with each line drawn
on the youths' arms

The heart of the country
pumping with opium
Burst arteries
where whole villages fell
Now called the place
of orphans and widows

Pressure rising higher
for elected officials
to save them
Prevent the death counts
from rising
or rather cover up
the ones already done

Looking for reprieve
among other countries
But reprieve found them
in the form of a
hallowed out
ballpoint pen

DELUSIONS OF PRIVILEGE

Dragging your hand across ribs
until your collar
The sound of hunger
running between the b o n e s
Drinking the the brown gutter slop
watching your skin turn *putrid*
helpless against the thirst
Losing an ey or a l mb or a fi ger
being thankful your life still holds

You run your hands along your pockets for change
and find a slight *sag* in weight
Fearing that you'll turn thief to thief's victim
you scramble home to give it to your mother
who goes and extends those t r a c k s on her arms
and when she runs out of petty change
she'll find the old creepy men
and exchange in the streets' coin
While she files away her life
you'll wander the dark alleys
not fearing the kidnappers that lurk
for who would want a boy
   so dirty
      so malno rished
         so unbelievably p or
No – they'll pick the young plump girls
and sell them to the highest bidder
so sitting here means

not having to sell yourself
Body and soul
It means you have
f o o d
water
shelt r

SEVEN SIBLINGS

Fighting with brothers
for scrapes of land
Land that only has
a couples years of fertility left

Praised favourites getting the deed
The smart getting educations
Leaving homes behind
Saying bye for the last time

All in a fight for decaying earth
Floods and laws already
killing what wasn't worth
killing relationships for

WHO ARE THE SCUTTLING RATS?

Standing above a garbage pit
piled on the side of the road
Right there
– among the wrappers for
plastic bags
imported shampoo bottles
and discarded pads –
are countless needles
Far from detritus

A young man grabs ahold
of the syringe
avoiding the sharp edge
Slightly shadowed
yet still in sight
he unbuckles
his belt
Rushes to pull each hole
past the threadbare loops
Ties it around his arm
Bites hard
– not unsimilar to the rats
scattering below –
and jabs down
Still standing above a pile
on the side of the road

26

NUMBERS DON'T COLLUDE WITH VICTORY

Ten teachers
share a message to a continent
Using books and swords
to find their warriors
in the enemies' ranks
Those not reading
still absolved with water
when the battle ends

Twenty one soldiers
rise on a marching army
of twenty four thousand
Not fleeing behind fences
but standing strong
amongst the battle fort walls
Blending in a white man's uniform
still carrying a Sikh's heart proud

One man
against a country of one billion
Left alone in a state no longer his
Motherland sectioned off
with paper flags

We've been fighting forevermore
foreigners trying to kill
our warriors
Yes their bodies now ash
but their presence walks among us
because for all the attempts
you can't kill fighting spirits

27

IN THE NAME OF GANDHI

A friend of the common man
asked me to put down my arms
to stop protecting a son
an ailing father
In the name of progress
stop fighting the goddamned gavel
They'll quote that bald aging man
Saying the golly old
"peace prosper and save the land"

Imagine if you had what he has
People who lived and worshiped
to even touch his hand
A man with others to take the fall
can climb as high as he wants
Hands to grab
Others to push down
Still people scrambling for bodies to pile

They'll build that never ending staircase
that spirals on and on
That with a squint and a tilt
starts to look a bit like a podium
So higher and higher it grows
higher and higher the body count goes
Astounding for an uncommon man
holding no arms of his own
Perhaps a glance at the arms he steps on
tells the tale

TIMELINE

Are we a singular line drawn
with jagged points standing out
Labelling "two thousand dead"
and the "start of the end"

Not enough room on this timeline
for those shines of happiness
though the stiff sharpie
Too insignificant to be written down
so mold the singular line that is us

I meet another person
who asks for the story of us
I show the timeline
with it's jagged depressing increments
They point to the spaces
between the points
and I respond
that I don't remember

HAIR

One strand over
Another strand back
All the way down
Till it hits a rubber band

Mother braids
Sister braids
You braid back
All the way down
Till it hits a rubber band

Weave it with the wind
Weave it with the bells
Weave it with love
So it jingles when
The rope is thrown down

Tapestry
Ancestry
It all is the same
Pretty threads
Lovely heads
They both hold a sway

One strand over
Another strand back
All the way down
Till it hits a rubber band

SOUL OF PUNJAB

Where aught lie
the soul of Punjab?
Is it not among the mustard fields
with rivulets flowing through the stalks
Or is it among the drying grass
Burning beneath the summer sun

Take the soil out of our blood
Take the soul out of Punjab
Broken tongues and distant nations
disjointed in recollection

Don't wash your hands
of the dirt that makes our land
For from the dirt we rose
as the five rivers ran

Placing us in a weighted palm
Five fingers interclasped

2001: The Mussalmans

The September 11th terrorist attacks cemented
islamophobia in American history, but
the first victim of hate crime was a Sikh named Balbir
Singh Sodhi. There are over
300 reported hate crimes against Sikhs in the first month
after 9/11. Personal accounts
suggest the number is far higher.

vengeful twins strike down
silk turbans left in rubble
smoke cleared long ago

MAPS

They're taught to look at Canada
Memorize its many
provinces and territories
Learn the culture of
Surrey
  Brampton
    Abbotsford
Understand how to get
to the grocery store
though it lies
thousands of miles away

So when you hand them
a puzzle
with cut out states
and capitals on flags
They struggle to even
place their own
in the right spot
Looking like children
who struggle to match
simple rhyming words
Putting *map*
next to *ran*

CANADIAN TAX

I come here and pay my dues
Taking bribes and strikes
aimed at immigrants
All while they have the audacity
to go on strike
for an extra weekend holiday

Then I learn that the tax we pay
goes to settlers just like us
Thousands in property tax
for land they stole

The jobs we allegedly steal
nonexistent in a perfect world
Pumping oil out of the ground
to top drums
Lugging trucks full of plastic
across borders
Scrubbing an ice machine
at the gas stop
Disrupting the picture
of Canada before

THE YOUNG PRINCES

There was a young prince not 6 years old
He wore a silk crown void of gold
From the land of the brave
The land that was lost
The boy may have been young
But coward he was not

He practiced his faith with fierce conviction
But the red and blue flags came
Ripping clasped hands apart
Placing bibles into bruised palms
On a mission to hunt them all
Until they saw the mighty land fall

The prince was but a child
Absorbing what he was taught
Brought up in the cold castles
Learning to eat with frigid metal
The same yellow rod
replaced the pretty silk

Delicate weaving hands slapped away
By calloused ones twisting in a hearth
Chains prattling attempting to recreate
But the ring on his head rang empty
Hollow is as hollow seems
Gold only a sign of thievery
Across the seven seas
The one mistaken for thee

A prince with a feathered crown lay
Wolves howled to the moon
The earth drummed beneath his feet
Nature's sound a touch offbeat

They stripped his sounds away
Hammers replaced the harmonies
Placing nails down into the perfect smile
Attaching tragedies to withered souls
Blood merging their jesuit rings
With the warriors' weathered bones

Nature's voice was stolen
Precious soils sifted through
They hoped to leave with filled pockets
But left behind empty hearts
Hollow is as hollow seems
Gold only a sign of thievery

PRICE OF BLOOD

We're beaten down and down
What do we get?
What price is paid for the blood we spilled?
What reward is given for being leaders on expeditions?

Left to scrape together change
for bandages
Forgotten
until our strength is
needed for another war
that they started

Yet we will respond to the call for change
No price too small
for being the example of courage

PAINT ME WITH THE COLOURS OF THE RAINBOW

Women walking on sidewalks in black
No longer wearing the vibrant colours
that are ours
The red orange and yellow
bleached from blouses
Jeans a dull denim blue
instead of a range from green to indigo

The combination of pigments
has never been black
The accumulation at the end
when laid to flames as vibrant
as the lives before then

Moreover a blank space
for colour in the next
Paint prepped for the canvas
So paint me with the colours
of the rainbow
when it is my time to go
and I will go with a smile
that shines light on the funeral

CAST ME IN A PLAY

Clear for local dispatch.
On the lookout for 6 foot South Asian male with cast on
arm

I look down at my cast
Littered with names
Manjeet
Deep
Jassi...

3 hours earlier

The stadium roars with thrown objects and swears
A miniature version of the largest match
Pakistan v. India
Instead of the hot humid weather
the nutmeg tones stand out on snow

Manjeet just cleared from a mechanics exam
Our star player ready to send the other team
straight back to our continent

An arm winds up ready to throw
a ball that scorches up that snow
Alas out of the white landscape
come slightly less pale figures
Swaggering up as if they own the field
Not far from the truth
since they belong of this pasty dirt

far more than we do

But this cricket match is our reign
and property be damned if they interrupt
the greatest match of the centu– the semester

I imitate their swagger and stroll my way down
The crowd parting like the Red Sea
awaiting my standoff with the intruders

All eyes on me
and my recently acquired cast
that people clamoured over for a pen
just to scrawl names on the paper maché

Not one person notices the batter
firing up
invigorated by my theatrical display
Not one person notices
the slight lift of his arm
Not even when that bat rises up
and WHACK
slams against the foreman's head

WHITE SEA

The white sea comes to
play on my toes
Compared to the brown sand
a gracious color

My feet lift off
Separating from solid ground
A wade into the calm
Floating in the middle of the world
Then a tide washes over
and the undercurrent sweeps in
Pushing me out to the depths

I see the tiger's shark equivalent
and the daunting blue whales
All of us minding on another
Our true fear
lies in the abyss below
The pressure tightens
as it pulls me deeper in
I turn my hand to my face
to see sparing pockets of air
freed to the surface

Nevertheless
the white sea washes over
Not heeding a single soul
So I watch my legs dissolve
No longer able to fight

for my glimpse of freedom

Schools of fish pass by
Clusters of children following mothers
Corals stretch
Embracing one another

I have become one
with this white sea
Caught in a current
when I only wanted
to swim

LITTLE INDIA

Little India isn't
in the cluttered streets
with half english signs
It's in our homes
when relatives gather

Family functions
for every birthday
celebration
and government holiday

Collected dishes
overflowing from
appetizers to dessert
Beers propped open
before barbeques

Little India lies in
tired guests
passing out on our
three beds pressed together
One master
and two twins

Separate rooms immaterial
Why basement suites
get converted to houses for twelve
Not accustomed to the separation
of walls between
sleeping quarters
and shops indoors

LANGAR HALL

Little ones stumbling by
carrying cups
Followed by elder siblings
carrying jugs

Teenagers apprenticing mothers
Their ovals less like circles
Their squares more like trapezoids

Awkward young men and women
Attempt to coordinate limbs
For control of ladles and serving bowls

Elders on pension funds
sharing news in the back
Reminding the young ones
to wash their hands

ADRIFT PAPERS TO GLUE

A generation's glue
Holding together loose
                    family
              threads

Calling every birthday
Attending every funeral
Leading the fight on aging
                    and severing
              bonds

Mocked for the devout efforts
of phoning hours on end
but they are the ones
we keep in our heart
for they are the ones
insuring our children
are not raised apart

WHERE ELSE, IF NOT HOME

Where else will you see
a crow perched on a cow
Its beak raised in silence
to its large partners vow

Where else will you hear
the bustle of hustlers
Fighting over honks of horns
Street littered with electrics poles

The shops range all sizes
The only common traits are
skin colour pants are brown
and hands are for passing rupees

ELECTRICAL FAILURES

Flicking a switch
to allow the tap to heat
Hopping in amidst the steam
but the water tank runs out
in the middle of a shower
Yelling down at your sister
to turn on the generator
Knowing you should have
used a bucket and pitcher

Eating dinner
when the lights go out
Walking outside to enjoy
okra under the stars
Blistering hot days of summer
more of a struggle
nevertheless mosquito nets prepped
Switching out ice fans
for the faint breeze

NEWSPAPER CLIPPINGS

Excerpt from Punjabi Tribune
Found in Advertisements

Twenty-year old Simran is looking for a potential husband!
Father, Inderjit Singh, is searching for a potential match in mid-
to-late twenties. The candidate must be clean-shaven Jatt and a
practicing Sikh. Preferably a doctor that permanently resides in
Canada.

Want to know more about Simran?
- She is fair-skinned and beautiful *(image featured below)*
- Weighing fifty four kgs and tall at one-hundred-and-seventy cm
- High school graduate aiming to complete a Bachelor's in Accounting
- Currently has Permanent Residence in Canada
- Father, Inderjit Singh, is reputable farmer in Ludhiana, Punjab and is of considerable wealth
- From a large family with 3 siblings. Brother, Amandeep Singh, is a highly successful self-employed businessman residing in Vancouver, Canada,

If interested, please contact Inderjit Singh at: +91 6543-99734
Let's find your match today!

*Note that the above is a work of fiction

ARRANGED

My husband and I
stumbled across a home
While beautiful
it was full of doors
He touched a knob
Fell down a staircase
One moment there
another gone

I grieved when he fell
However he soon returned with
a tiny girl
in a white dress
holding two chalices
I was supposed to drink
from the white
Him the black

Once we were absolved
and drank our share
we sent her back
carrying the two empty chalices
down the stairs

She came every once awhile
Coming to trust us
Dining with us
Playing with dolls
Wearing clothes from

a room that looked like
it was opened for her

One day
a man comes up with her
Tells us to clean her up
Bleach the blood out
of the dress
Put cream on the scars
that lie under

We sob
The cheer bleached from the home
because that tiny girl
was telling us she's our daughter
and we finally listened
With no absolution
we refuse to
send her down that staircase
instead throwing down the choices
Spilling the empty chalices

BOUQUET OF BLACK ROSES

The bruise a black rose
blooms across her face
Look how large it is
under its master's care

Tilt your head –
see the petal folds
Her red eye
the centerpiece of it all

It's a gift she
keeps to herself
The average not ready
for its complexity

So she covers up
the black and blue
The painting replaced
by her natural hue

A streak mars the illusion
as a tear slides down
In awe that yes
pain *is* beauty

SIGNATORY OF MAN'S COUNTRY

Always a grandfather's glass pupil
not her grandmother's little poet
Unable to sign

Always a father's delicate doll
not the child her mother raised with restrain
Unable to sign

The plaque on their house
with masculine names
Property bought and owned by two
Only one side littering legal papers
Passport holding no value
when a man's word
lies down the block
exchanging empty sentences
for stamp purview

CHANDIGARH

I look around me and all I see is
government clones wearing turbans
Running their own tiny corrupt empires
Giving them numbers
Calling them districts

They call you to their castles for tea
Show off their flock of chickens
You leave unsure the shrieks
come from the flapping hens
or outside the steel studded fence

The clones mock the children sent here
Laughter rumbling over manicured lawns
as they start off stumbling over their tongues
Soon enough the children's laughter will
merge with the echoes over artificial hills
Speaking the language they learned
Forgetting the language they built

BOOK TOMB

Searching tombs of books
for skulls of those lost
Looking for answers in faces
belonging to heads long gone

Failing to find the dead
in our literature
History scraped
by years of uneducation
in our youth
and lack of passion for the pen
Expecting oral stories
to preserve the minute details
or keep it unmuddled
by opposing views

Leaving outsiders
to write the insider's point of view
Trusting our history
in foreign hands

IRON BRANDING OR ROPE HANGING

We ran from
nooses hanging in village centers
blood stains in front of studded gates
bodies thrown atop mass pyres
Here we get chosen
hunted
and tied down just the same

A small triumph
that instead of being left
with thread
and a forlorn family
we're left with
a brand
burned into skin
Fire now for the living
cold hearts now belonging
to the white man's grave

Money still grabbed from
our pockets
Gangs the same
Just dealing in
dollars instead of rupees

GALI FLOODS

/ˈɡʌli/ ·a narrow passage behind or between buildings

A small stoop that separates the garden
from our collected shoes
Using brooms to push it outside
Water spilling through the bristles

Flowing down into the gali
Passing the homes raised and
remade with overflowing pockets
sinking into the garbage pits
carrying plastic into

People with buckets prepped
Knowing the exchange for the low cost
of living underground

The buckets pull brown sludge out
It rushes back in and through
continuing down the gali
with rickshaws taking shoppers
over large puddles
The soaking fabric failing
to protect the assemblage of clothes

The bills stay dry
tucked under seats and pillows

PROMOTIONS

They show me the physiotherapy room first
The donor's money evident in those halls
The patients perk up as I come in
The speaker I bring for dancing
a great break from mundane spinning
round and round on the elliptical

I spend most of the time drinking tea
Colluding with doctors
on the gentle administration of pills
and chatting about relatives
while flies buzz around our covered cups

Soon I get promoted to the top floor
More sun
But the bars for walls
more confining
Each day logged
by the twist of the key in a hole
The nurse letting me in recognizing
my expensive cut of cotton
and the unshorn braids

There we play airplanes
Colouring with crayons
Giggling when I mark them all 10s
More excited than anyone I've ever seen
for lesson plans
Yelling 123s on cue

Applause at the end
My bubbly personality
a welcome reprieve
from sleeping around the clock
waking exactly thrice for meals
The sun streaming through those bars
allowing drowsiness
– an easy out for boredom

I'm promoted to the role of sister
Thought my youngest student
is pushing past my age
by at least fifteen

2 months in
I'm shown the last corridor
Graduating past all 3 floors
This has all 4 walls concrete
I discover soon there's no need for bars
My lessons have no attendance
saving the 5 that double as caretakers
As I walk into the rooms
to retrieve my students
a musty space is found

I discover
many in diapers
splayed on blankets
Confined by the edges of the fraying thread
Surrounded by nothing
but those four walls and a singular bed

All my blind students
collated here
No one willing to show them
the touch of grass
The only texture
they feel is concrete on their feet
when they call a nurse
to guide them to the bath

A couple strips of cloth
tie two of them
to the window
Deemed too rowdy
to be included in
the empty schedule
of nothing

One confused child
in a woman's body
remains confined to the blanket's range
Sitting in a pool of piss and sweat
The diaper expected to regulate

This child sheds tears every day
The only sound coming from that room
her asking to phone her papa
Nobody reminding her
that we found them on the street

THE GARBAGE MAN

The garbage man only
travels one street
Grabbing bags of trash
that lie on the haveli's
front door

Piling it up
on the back of their
assorted vehicles
Turning one corner
and dumping it right there
in front of
the servants' homes

2020: The Canadians

The farmer's protest in India was the one the largest protests in history. It was in opposition to three bills proposed by Parliament that threatened farmers' livelihoods in Punjab and the surrounding states. The bills were successfully overturned on November 19, 2021. This was largely in part due to the global demonstration of support.

cannons hit our youth
elders pull swords from scabbards
steel verses oceans

SILENCE SONGS

All the stars in Bollywood
inspired by their home's fields
Using Switzerland instead
Abandoning the roots of their plants
Singing in a mix of languages
from their northern region
including Urdu and Punjabi
Still using subtitles
listed as Hindi

Academics at the top of their game
but covering the Singh in their name
Putting down kirpans
for success as entrepreneurs
Claiming scientific process
eliminates the need
for individuality

Actors
Academics
All attributed to success by virtue
yet failing to use the accrued credit
to support the families
that paid for their stardom in change
Continuing to use
the beauty of the land
and the handpicked values
A deemed necessary task for certain
to gain approval
of the their disparaging bosses

WAIT FOR HER TO STAND

She was only 5 foot 7 inches
an awkward height for a dainty girl
When she sat in chairs
she would unfold her limbs
perch on the furthest edge
to extend the reach of her toes
curl her upper half
the imaginary string for posture erased
replaced by the crunch of a zipper
Her frame closing as if
the room closed on her

But my god!
When she stood
unfurled those gangly limbs
elongated those legs hiding under
those 5 foot 7 inches
seemed inexplicably tall
undoubtedly regal
The room remained too small
but this standing girl would
reach and stretch
for who was to confine her

OLD RIVERS FLOW IN BLOOD

The battlefield was their altar
Swords pressed with honour and religion
Laying tributes of their own

That red trickled down
From their wayward graves
Crying rivers for newborn babes

They see the descendants
Praying for the forgotten dead
Remembering their comrades

Those salt filled tears
Create tracks on the altar
Making mockery of crimson

For the slight hand of water
Cleans cobblestone stains
Burning the long closed scars

TEXTBOOK ANSWERS

I can recount all the tales of greek gods
List their roman counterparts
though I'm technically monotheist
Believing in only one God

I know more of Christianity than anything else
Can list the names and records of
Cain and Abel
Adam and Eve
Moses and Aaron
and those far more obscure

I know the intricate history
of colonialism in Europe
Approaching it from a place
of remorse and regret
Never feeling the rage and sorrow of
my predecessors being
the conquest

I feel asleep to my grandmother's folk tales
yet somehow when asked
I only recall
"Old Macdonald"
and the egg that sat on a wall
Education even touching
the memories of a two year old

PROPORTIONS

A mere 0.38%
in world of billions
Not large enough
to be added to a curriculum
or be remembered as more
than the men in turbans

Yet look at our members
Literature, politics, military
Topping every career
Love in our steps
Passion in our bones
Religion in our blood
not a temple

Raised in flat fields
Trained to jump
from impossible heights

NOVEMBER 11TH

Carrying poppies on pins
Seeing
   Canadians
      Americans
        British
Showcasing their troops
Billboards filled with pale faces
Not recognizing my heritage should
also be represented

My great grandfather
drank poisoned water in Burma
Fighting the
       Japanese

My lineage traced
To the first Great War
Against
   Germans
      Hungarians
        Bulgarians

My ancestors
ashes never got returned
Spread across battlefield grounds
Ingraining a fear
That our courage and bravery
are traded for disrespect and
neglect that we belong
   among *the remembered*

GHUNTAS

My name doesn't exist in english
Yes – there's a U, a T and an A
but the U isn't quite a U
Falling somewhere between there
and a double O
Plucking notes that go unpicked
by an untrained ear
The T could be called a TH
yet it's not as soft
The hard tones
need a drastic change in tongues
The A most definitely
isn't the one listed in the English alphabet
instead following the melodic pattern
of my original accent

That's alright
I'll give a person 3 tries
One for each foreign letter

But my kindness and forgiveness
is already forgotten
for the second and third
The garbled sounds stuck
on their tongue
Still it's quite alright
I understand that english
chose to abstain from certain letters
The phonetic alphabet being

a pick-and-choose buffet table
My name picking up the scraps

So I let my name
switch countless hands
until the only correct memory
is what remains on the hospital bed

KHALISTAN

I see my community
protesting around me
disrupting religion for outrage
Yellow flags mounted on shoulders
Yelling louder than the prayers

They forget
we are Sikh
Meant not to defend just ourselves
but everyone
That includes our adopted siblings
in the country we became
Albeit forced to share grace
protecting everyone just the same

They forget
1947
When creating borders
created animosity
Trains of death
would become planes
in the modern age

Promote kindness
Fight for equality
Don't allow discrimination
to make us enemies
ignoring the plea
of common humanity

MIGHTY

Leave us in our small space
in our small corner of the world
where we refuse to pull people in
Small or big faith no matter
when you remember that the only value
is being a human

Pursuit of faith
pursuit of God
is a pursuit of ethics
So yes – we may stay small
or shrink smaller still
but we refuse to accept a convert
Coerced by deception and false faith
We accept a believer
who sees a small religion
that's faith has held true

CHANDIGARH, PART 2

Tourists in our own city
Viewing plates with
    Hiryana
    Himachal Pradesh
    CH for *Chandigarh*
all states that used to be one
Blatantly stated on the front of our motor
Punjab – the original founder
What once was a sign
to wave friendly
Now a sign to wave down
pull over to the side
Extra points for symbols
swinging behind the mirror

They'll walk up
with a baton swinging by their side
and threats of jail time under their belt
Expecting to stroll away
with a couple hundred bucks
So you'll small talk
in the government tongue
Say "thank you officer"
but trying to say
"We were once brothers"

DREAMING OF DELHI

Terrified of Delhi
Seeing the news broadcasts
of women pillaged and assaulted
on the streets they call home
Seeing posts of travellers
followed with leering eyes
Men watching their every step
Visiting hundreds of place
yet Delhi is what strikes fear
when single and alone

Having dreams
conjured by subconscious
combining the stories expressed
of turning onto an overcast street
to avoid traffic
Stopping when
a seemingly dead body
stalls the road
Slamming the brakes
as you should
but robbers jumping out
of the shadows
Taking anything
– anything –
they want
from the prey they caught

SUNDIALS

Sun looming above
denoting 3pm
on the half moon curving up
It's larger twin out of commission
Stairs leading up
sectioned off with velvet ropes
The twelve pillars around
still open to public attraction
from cancer to capricorn

Tourist oohing and aahing
Thinking it as personality definer
One of confirmation bias
Not realizing this is a decider of fates
Success or the hard rock of failure
Marriage or the companion of loneliness
Life or the embrace of suffocation

Miniature versions
lie in priest's office
Name plaques leaning on them
instead of stairs
Their desk job
the task of playing God's hand
Praising the stars
yet only sparing them a glance
The real fortune already decided
before the dawn's break

THE MOOSE CRAZE

1 week
   1 month
     1 year
after his death
the speakers still blast
The craze still going
News blogs dedicated to current events
still displaying the fans' reverence

I listened to his music
Was in awe of his performance
A representative of Punjabi influence

Alas the craze a coverup
Strong beats playing at election booths
Sites interspersing the current deaths
with the onslaught of old news

Still stalking a grieving father
Producing tears for the mass media
Ignoring the cries of fathers
who beg propaganda to
save their sons from
the noose
  the chopping block
    the electrical chair

His lyrics
talking of the slaughter our youth

and the political deaths of our country
tuned out
for the trumpets of his funeral

SOURCE MATERIAL

An old woman sits on the ground below me
The appropriate position for mopping floors
I lounge on my plush chair
arms hanging over
legs tucked in
Looming over me is my grandfather
supremacy established through standing

Remember the lessons the teacher showed
Placing his feet towards a book of old days
Pouring water in the direction opposite the sun
yet we places books with scripture on pedestals
Forgetting God is everywhere
Not watching His graced books
but marking the sin of not offering chairs to elders

SOCIAL SCALE

My brother is the most important

I know this in the way
my grandmother picked him
at the slightest sign of separation

In the way
my sister and I's countless awards
collected dust high on the shelf
while he was applauded
for getting to graduation

My brother is the most important

I know this in the way
my aunt had four kids
before cutting tubes
The first three being girls
Dresses not as cute

In the way
my cousin managed her family's taxes
but *he* took all the withdrawals
Her saving up countless dollars
to buy a car after public transport
but a shiny key waiting for her brother
though he crashed his last drunk

I know this in the way
that the bartenders
slip the brothers
sloshing beer at weddings
while we still do our rounds
of graciously greeting guests
Our mothers yelling
to straighten our backs
to show grace in the quiet
Unless it's to gossip about relatives
or comment on the snacks

It's women choosing the boys
Gasping when the cake revealed blue
then asking why they get degraded
and beat blue

My brother is the most important
It's not his fault
He's a sweet kid
but I just wait and watch
for those signs of aggression
– to realize those privileges

Scared for the day
he raises his hand
Creating full circle
Causing his wife to pray to God
that her singular X chromosome
somehow cooperates

SILK SHACKLES

Shackles have turned into silk ribbon
ignoring the lioness's cries
the roars that reverberate through years
carrying the anguish of wars satisfied

My freedom is my prisoner of war
held tightly against my chest
The rewards the lioness reaped from battles
she fought alongside men

The shortening of a skirt, the show of an ankle
Call it Rebellion if you wish just be sure to
watch me play with these kittens called boys
watch me pull each thread of the ribbon away

THE CRIMES OF MOTHERS' MOUTHS

Naivete, it's always caused people
to look funny at me
A woman's body, a child's mind
"Grow up and view your life!"
There's the beggar
      There's the thief
All looking to steal something precious from me

So churn up the dirt and the grime
Clean my window with mud
Shove gruesome pictures into my sight
Feed me with the filth

Still there lies the beggar
      There sits the thief
Not a hand lifted
      nor a foot shifted
Yet my most precious gift
has been stolen from me

FAMILY BUSINESS

Meddling in affairs
a family business
with scheduled times
for interventions
Held with far reaches of family
An extended cousin
twice removed
barging in

Plans made within whispers
Adding more bodies
to an already sweaty room
Furnace cranked high
with illuminated voices
Exhilarated by
arguments falling on new ears

Proclamations made
in the heat of the moment
Suitcase packed by the side
of the front door
A threat all too recurring

Regulated breaks
for drinks to squelch the thirst
and the hot anger rising up
The accountant struggling to
keep track of records
and taxes overdue

DIZZY SPELLS

Someone on the street
calls for change
You pass without a second thought
A twinge of guilt collides later
creeping up your shoulders
Spinning the thought
you think to turn around
Making you dizzy
Stopping your pause

By then
the walk too long
Enough not to waste
the seconds back
As if the time of the wealthy
worth more than pennies
to a homeless man

While you leave the steps behind
the dizzy spells follow
You start wondering
the headaches that plague your parents
– presumptuously by headaches
and the workings of the working man –
perhaps are caused by a lack of kindness
despite lessons spilling down
from seemingly righteous baring

TWO PEAS OUT OF A POD

Taking tomatoes from the vine
Picking peas out of a pod
Peeling tiny pieces of garlic
as a little collector

Handed a pin heavier
than my head
Standing on my stool
rolling perfect circles

She'll pat me on the back and
thank me
Then take my misshapen circle
to roll it back into form

She'll pass me the spoon
Ask me to watch the pot
and I'll dutifully stare
Watch it simmer and stir

That tub of colours will be pulled
from the nearest shelf
It's long journey shown in
the shelf lining art

The spoon will be blown
held it out for my taste
My opinion holding the greatest value

in her esteemed viewpoint

Finally, she'll ask me to run along
my knees more able
Call the entire family
to the dining table

We'll sit down
Enjoy our familiar feast
and I'll tell all who will listen
that I was her little aide

TO MY FATHER

You tell me a story

Through your colour
                    your texture
                             your cracks
Through the steady
   drip
of your tears
Through the shuddering of the ground
caused by your sobs

You tell me a story
Through these new eyes
– eyes I wished never to see
The storybook is meant to be flipped
with me: the author
and you: the audience

You're supposed to be
the foundation of our home
Nature's beauty unable to flourish
without the rock that
plants fold their bodies around,
critters use as nurturing nests and
life creates miracles through
— birth to death

However
you are made of the same
soil and sand
as me
Just compacted over time

Smooth
    Polished
        Perfect
That's what others and I see
Not understanding that
It's a result of
centuries of pain and pressure
of being compressed by water
    and the   of responsibility
                weight

Hardened by weather
Beaten down by the Great Mother
All working towards gaining your submission
to the laws of the land

Even Mother is often wrong
She doesn't comprehend that
you are allowed to crack
to let your pain escape through slivers
not to pollute your surroundings
or me
but to the vast unknown
Lost in the current of our natural world

So perhaps you need my ear
not my eyes
Not to take a peak and scamper
at the prospect of fear
but to *listen*

So I listen
   to the story your tears told

PTSD

In the western world
whispers surround us
Calling out the word "depression"
but that name falsehood
My condition in actuality
only takes numbers
Four that spell out
forty years of terror

For in 1984
you needed to be fire
in order to stay planted
among the wind and ash
The consequence?
My lips burned shut
by the burning
of history's lapse

But child
your birth was clear of smoke
so write with your clear conscious
Just be sure to write in red pen
Spin the words
already present
in my journal's text

My fight was 1984
to be sure I was heard
Yours is to make sure
our descendants hear the echoes

Bonus Content

ਟੁੱਟੀ ਪੰਜਾਬੀ

Original

ਸੁਣੋ ਮੇਰੀ ਟੁੱਟੀ ਪੰਜਾਬੀ
ਜੇੜੀ ਮੈਂ ਇਕ ਇਕ ਸ਼ਬਦ ਬੋਲਦੇ ਹੈ

ਦਿਖਾਓ ਮੈਨੂੰ
ਹੌਲੀ ਹੌਲੀ
ਤੇ ਸਿਖਾਓ ਮੈਨੂੰ
ਮੇਰੀ ਮਾਂ ਬੋਲੀ

ਤੇ ਮੇਰੇ ਤੇ ਹਾਸੇ ਵੀ
ਮਜ਼ਾਕ ਕਰੋਲੋ
ਕੀ ਇਹ ਕੁੜੀ
ਕੀ ਕੁਝ ਬਲੋਦੀ ਸੀ
ਤੇ ਮੈਂ ਚੁੱਪ ਚਾਪ ਬੈਠਕੇ
ਸੁਣਲੋ ਗਾਈ

ਪਰ ਫਿਰ ਹਾਸਾ ਹੌਲੀ
ਹੋਜੇਗੇ

ਸਿਰਫ ਮੇਰੀ ਅਵਾਜ ਰਹਿ ਗਈ

ਤੇ ਤੁਸੀਂ

ਕੰਨ ਬੰਧ ਕਰੋ ਗਏ

ਫਿਰ ਕੌਣ ਸੁਣੂਗਾ ਮੇਰੀ ਟੁੱਟੀ ਪੰਜਾਬੀ

ਜੇੜ੍ਹੀ ਮੇਂ ਇਕ ਇਕ ਸ਼ਬਦ ਬੋਲਦੀ ਸੀ

ਤੇ ਕੌਣ ਲਿਖੂਗਾ

ਤੁਹਾਡੀ ਕਹਾਣੀ

ਇਕ ਇਕ ਸ਼ਬਦ

ਹੌਲੀ ਹੌਲੀ

ਕਾਗਜ਼ ਦੇ ਉੱਪਰ

ਤੁਹਾਡੇ ਬਚਿਆ ਦੀ ਪੰਜਾਬੀ

Bonus Content

TUTTI PUNJABI
Transcription

suno meri tuti punjabi
jaydee mei ek ek shabad bolde hai

dakhao meinu
hawlee, hawlee
te sakhao meinu
meri ma bolee

te meru te haso ve
mazak karlo
ke eh kudee
kee kush boldee see
te mai chup chap bait ke
sunlo gee

per fir hasa hawlee
hawjinge
sirf meri avaaj riauh gee
te tousee
kana bandh karo ge
fir kawn sunuga meri tuti punjabi
jaydi mei ek, ek shabad boldee see

te kawn likhuga
touhadee kihani
ek, ek shabad

hawlee, hawlee
kagz de uper,
touhade bachia de punjabi
Bonus Content

BROKEN PUNJABI
Translation

listen to broken punjabi mine
that I speak word by word

show me
slowly slowly
and teach me
my mother tongue

it's alright
laugh at me too
joke
say "this girl
what nonsense was she saying"
and I will silently sit
all while listening

but then the laughter
will quiet
only my voice will remain
and you
will close your ears
then who will listen to broken punjabi mine
which I was speaking word by word

and who will write
your story
word by word
slowly slowly
on paper
your children's punjabi

ਖਾਲੀ ਅਲਮਾਰੀ

Original

ਖਾਲੀ ਅਲਮਾਰੀ
ਸਿਰਫ ਕਮੀਜ਼ ਤੇ ਸਲਵਾਰ
ਆਪਣੀਆਂ ਕਿਤਾਬਾਂ ਕਿੱਥੇ ਹਨ
ਲੁਧਿਆਣੇ ਸੰਗਰੂਰ ਤੇ ਅੰਮ੍ਰਿਤਸਰ
ਦੀਆਂ ਗਲੀਆਂ ਵਿੱਚ
ਮਾਰਕਿਟ ਦੇ ਖੁੰਜੇ ਵਿੱਚ
ਇੱਕ ਬਾਬੇ ਦੀ ਦੁਕਾਨ
ਇੱਕ ਕਿਤਾਬ ਦੱਸ ਰੁਪਈਏ
ਤੇ ਬਾਬੇ ਲਈ ਗੱਲ ਬਾਤ
ਅਕਾਲਗੜ੍ਹ ਦੀ ਦੁਕਾਨ ਵਾਲੇ
ਸ਼ੈਲਫ ਤੋਂ ਸੌ ਲਹਿੰਗੇ ਖਿੱਚਦੇ
ਚਾਲੀ ਜੁੱਤੀਆ ਉੱਤੋਂ ਸੁੱਟਦੇ

ਮਨ ਪਰੇਸ਼ਾਨ
ਕਿ ਆਪਣਾ ਇਤਿਹਾਸ
ਹਿੰਦੁਸਤਾਨ ਮੋਹਰੇ ਬਣੂਗਾ ਪਰਹਾਸ
ਦਰਹਾਸ!

ਕਿ, ਉੱਨੀ ਸੌ ਚੁਰਾਸੀ
ਅਸਲ ਵਿੱਚ ਹੋਇਆ
ਨਹੀਂ ਮਨ ਦੀ ਰਚਨਾ

ਸਰਕਾਰੀ ਸਕੂਲ ਦੱਸਦੇ
ਆਪਣੀ ਲੜਾਈ ਮੁਸਲਮਾਨ
ਤੇ ਪਾਕਿਸਤਾਨ ਦੇ ਨਾਲ
ਅਸਲ 'ਚ ਲੜਾਈ ਹੈ
ਕਿ ਆਪਣੇ ਬੱਚਿਆਂ ਨੂੰ
ਸਿਖਾਉਣਾ ਚਾਹੀਦਾ ਹੈ

ਘਰ ਆਪਣਾ ਸਿਰ ਉੱਤੇ
ਸਿਰ ਦੇ ਵਿੱਚ ਦਿਮਾਗ
ਪਰ ਕੋਈ ਸੋਚ ਦਿਮਾਗ ਵਿੱਚ ਨਹੀਂ

ਆਪਣਾ ਸਰੀਰ
ਇੱਕ ਖਾਲੀ ਅਲਮਾਰੀ
ਗਿਆਨ ਦੀ ਥਾਂ
ਪਾਟੀਆਂ ਲੀਰਾਂ

96

Bonus Content

KHALI ALMAARI
English Transcription

Khali Almaari
Sirf kameez te salwaar
Apne kithab kithe han
Ludhiana sangrur te amritsar
Dea galiaa vich
Market de khunje vich
Ek babe de dukaan
Ek kithaab das rupee
Te babe lay gal baath
Akalgar de dukaan wale
Shelf to saw lenghe khichde
Chalee juthiaa utho sutde

Man parshaan
Ki apna eitihaas
Hindustan mure banuga parhaas
Darhaas!
Ki, unee saw churasee (1984)
Asal vich hoia
Nehi man dee rachnaa
Sarkaari school dasthe
Apnee ladaee mussalman
Te pakistaan de naal
Asal vich apnee ladaee hai
Ki apne bachiaa nu
Sikhauna chahida hai

Ghar apne sir uthe

Sir de vich dimaag
Par koi soch dimaag vich nehee

Apnee sereer
Ek khali almaari
Giaan de thaa
Pateeaa leeraa

Bonus Content

EMPTY CLOSET
English Translation

Empty closet
Only shirts and salwaar
Where are our books?
On the streets of
Ludhiana, Sangrur and Chandigarh
In the corner of the market
is an elder's shop
One book is ten rupees
and conversation for the elder
Akalgar's shopkeepers
pull one hundred lehengas from the shelf
Forty shoes thrown from above

People worried
that our history
will become a fool
in front of Hindustan
Doubt!
that 1984 really happened
not just a creation of the mind
The government schools say
our fight is with mussalmans
and pakistan
In reality, our fight is
that our children
should be taught

A house over your head

A mind in your head
but no thought in your mind
Our body is
an empty closet
In the place of knowledge
there are ripped clothes

Manufactured by Amazon.ca
Acheson, AB

11513766R00061